1920: THE AFTERMATH - EXAMINING THE ROARING START TO THE TWENTIES

The Turmoil of Transition: Understanding the Sociopolitical Changes in the Post-War World

D.R. T Stephens

S.D.N Publishing

ISBN: 9798854602013

Cover design by: Art Painter
Library of Congress Control Number: 2018675309
Printed in the United States of America

CONTENTS

GENERAL DISCLAIMER

This book is intended to provide general information to the reader on the topics covered. The author and publisher have made every effort to ensure that the information herein is accurate and up-to-date at the time of publication. However, they do not warrant or guarantee the accuracy, completeness, adequacy, or currency of the information contained in this book. The author and publisher expressly disclaim any liability or responsibility for any errors or omissions in the content herein.

The information, guidance, advice, tips, and suggestions provided in this book are not intended to replace professional advice or consultation. Readers are strongly encouraged to consult with an appropriate professional for specific advice tailored to their situation before making any decisions or taking any actions based on the content of this book.

The views and opinions expressed in this book are those of the author and do not necessarily reflect the official policy or position of any other agency, organization, employer or company.

The author and publisher are not responsible for any actions taken or not taken by the reader based on the information, advice, or suggestions provided in this book. The reader is solely responsible for their actions and the consequences thereof.

This book is not intended to be a source of legal, business, medical or psychological advice, and readers are cautioned to seek the services of a competent professional in these or other areas of expertise.

Readers of this book are advised to do their own due diligence when it comes to making decisions and all information, products, services and advice that have been provided should be independently verified by your own qualified professionals.

CHAPTER 1: A WORLD IN FLUX - GLOBAL OVERVIEW OF 1920

The year 1920 arose on the heels of unprecedented global upheaval. The entire world, it seemed, was poised on the brink of a new era, an era shaped by war's devastating aftermath, the reshaping of national boundaries, shifting ideologies, and burgeoning technologies.

The specter of the Great War, or World War I, loomed large over this new decade. Over 16 million lives were lost, and more than 20 million people were wounded in the destructive conflict that had concluded barely two years prior. The political map of Europe, once dominated by sprawling empires, was now a fragmented mosaic of new states, reflecting the seismic shifts brought by the war.

In the East, the Russian Civil War raged on, further complicating an already tumultuous political landscape. The Bolsheviks, under the command of Vladimir Lenin, fought to consolidate their power over the vast expanses of the former Russian Empire. The eventual formation of the Soviet Union, though still some years away, was being forged in the crucible of this brutal conflict.

In the West, the newly-signed Treaty of Versailles sought to establish a tentative peace. However, the punitive measures it imposed on the Central Powers, particularly Germany, sowed the seeds of resentment that would eventually grow into another global conflict.

Ireland, too, was embroiled in a struggle for independence from British rule, a conflict that would culminate in the partition of the island and the establishment of the Irish Free State. Farther east, the collapse of the Qing dynasty in China had ignited a power struggle between the Nationalist Kuomintang and the emerging Communist Party, signaling the dawn of the Chinese Civil War.

Across the Atlantic, the United States emerged relatively unscathed from the global conflict, transitioning from a debtor to a creditor nation and positioning itself as an emerging world power. However, the nation was grappling with its own domestic issues: the contentious ratification of the 19th Amendment granting women's suffrage, the beginning of the Prohibition era, and the economic roller coaster that characterized the post-war years.

In addition, the year 1920 saw the birth of the League of Nations, an intergovernmental organization aiming to maintain global peace - a testament to the high hopes and deep anxieties of the time.

Meanwhile, cultural and technological transformations were underfoot, changing the very fabric of everyday life. The rapid expansion of radio technology, the rise of silent films, and the birth of the Jazz Age were all testaments to an increasingly interconnected, modern world. In the realm of science, significant advancements were being made, especially in medicine, as the world tried to prevent future pandemics in the aftermath of the devastating Spanish Flu.

In the midst of this flux, societies and economies were forced to adapt, seek out new opportunities, and confront emerging challenges. The world of 1920 was characterized by its turmoil, its dynamism, and above all, its desire for renewal after a decade defined by war and disease. Indeed, the year 1920 was a threshold, a point of transition from the scars of the past to the promise of a new, if uncertain, future.

CHAPTER 2:
THE TREATY OF
VERSAILLES - ECHOES
OF THE GREAT WAR

The reverberations of the Great War were still echoing loudly as the world welcomed the year 1920. The primary instrument of that echo was the Treaty of Versailles, a document that sought to formalize the end of the conflict, but in reality, it opened the door to new tensions and sowed the seeds for another world war.

Signed on June 28, 1919, and being enacted on January 10, 1920, the Treaty of Versailles marked the official end of the state of war between Germany and the Allied Powers. However, the Treaty was far more than a mere diplomatic formality; it was the blueprint for a new world order envisioned by the victorious powers, particularly France, Britain, and the United States.

The Treaty sought to impose heavy reparations on Germany, the perceived instigator of the war, to compensate for the enormous damage inflicted on the Allies. Germany's military was severely restricted, and the country lost significant territory to its neighbors and the newly created states in Eastern Europe. The Rhineland was demilitarized, the Saar Basin was placed under French control, and the League of Nations mandates saw

Germany's overseas colonies redistributed among the victors.

However, the punitive terms of the Treaty became a source of national humiliation and economic distress for the Germans. The war guilt clause, which held Germany and its allies responsible for causing the war, deepened the sense of resentment. This punitive peace stirred anger and discontent, fueling extremist ideologies that would eventually lead to the rise of Nazism.

The consequences of the Treaty stretched beyond Germany. The redrawing of Europe's map, particularly the establishment of new nations along ethnic lines, created a host of new geopolitical tensions. The dissolution of the Ottoman Empire and the constitution of brand new states in the Middle East under European mandates added another layer of complexity to an already intricate international scenario.

The Treaty of Versailles also saw the birth of the League of Nations, an intergovernmental organization intended to prevent another devastating war by fostering cooperation and collective security. The League was the thought up by American President Woodrow Wilson, who envisaged it as a platform where international disputes could be resolved peacefully. However, the United States, ironically, did not join the League due to opposition in the Senate, substantially weakening the new organization's influence and effectiveness.

The Treaty of Versailles, in many ways, was emblematic of the post-war world's conflicting impulses in 1920: the longing for peace and stability and the desire for justice and retribution. Its ambitious aim to redraw the world map and establish a new international order, sadly, only laid the groundwork for further conflict. The echoes of the Great War continued to resonate throughout the 1920s and beyond, amplified by the profound changes instigated by the Treaty of Versailles.

CHAPTER 3: RISE OF THE SOVIET UNION - THE BOLSHEVIK REVOLUTION CONTINUES

In the post-war world of 1920, the winds of change were blowing from the East, particularly from the vast territories of Russia. The year marked a critical juncture in the formation of the Soviet Union as the Bolshevik revolution continued to evolve, shifting the world's geopolitical landscape significantly.

After the 1917 abdication of Tsar Nicholas II, Russia was thrown into a chaotic period of political upheaval, culminating in the October Revolution led by Vladimir Lenin and the Bolshevik Party. With a vision to establish a communist society based on the principles of Marxism, the Bolsheviks seized control of the government, promising the Russian people' Peace, Land, and Bread.'

However, their rise to power was not uncontested. The Russian Civil War, a bloody conflict between the Red Army (Bolsheviks) and the White Army (a loose coalition of anti-Bolshevik forces), raged from 1918 to 1922. Despite facing numerous challenges, by 1920, the Red Army was gaining a decisive upper hand.

Under the leadership of Leon Trotsky, the Red Army utilized innovative tactics and leveraged the widespread desire for peace among war-weary peasants and workers to gradually wear down the White forces. By the end of 1920, the Bolsheviks had effectively taken control of most of the former Russian Empire.

While the war on the battlefield was being won, another battle was being fought on the economic front. In 1920, Lenin introduced the concept of "War Communism," aimed at maintaining the Red Army's supplies and combating economic crises. This policy centralized the production and distribution of goods, abolished private trade, and requisitioned surplus from the peasants. However, War Communism led to widespread discontent among the populace, and it exacerbated economic hardships, culminating in the famine of 1921.

Simultaneously, efforts were underway to reshape the political structure of the country. In 1920, the Russian Socialist Federative Soviet Republic was formally recognized as a federation, and the process of creating a new constitution commenced. The groundwork was being laid for the formation of a union of Soviet republics.

On the international front, the Bolsheviks were making efforts to spread the revolution beyond their borders. The Comintern, also known as the Third International, was an organization initiated in 1919 by Lenin to advocate for global communism. In 1920, at its second congress, the Comintern adopted the '21 Conditions,' which outlined the prerequisites for any European socialist party willing to join.

The events of 1920 were pivotal in the evolution of the Bolshevik Revolution and the rise of the Soviet Union. The Russian Civil War, the implementation of War Communism, and the endeavors to define a new political structure marked a profound shift in Russia's trajectory, with far-reaching implications for the rest of the world. As the year drew to a close, the ripples of this revolution continued to reverberate globally, a testament to the turmoil of transition that characterized the post-war world.

CHAPTER 4: THE IRISH WAR OF INDEPENDENCE - A NATION'S STRUGGLE FOR AUTONOMY

In the aftermath of the Great War, while nations grappled with reshaping boundaries and peace treaties, a notable conflict was brewing in the western reaches of Europe. The year 1920 marked a seminal point in Ireland's struggle for independence, a fight that had been simmering for centuries against one of the world's superpowers: Britain.

The Irish War of Independence, also referred to as the Anglo-Irish War, was a guerrilla war waged by the Irish Republican Army (IRA) opposing the British government and its armed forces in Ireland. The war spanned from January 1919 to July 1921 but saw some of its most intense and transformative events in the year 1920.

The year began under the shadow of the Soloheadbeg Ambush, which occurred in January 1919. It was a critical event that marked the start of the war, pushing the Irish cause into a new, more violent phase. This momentum continued into 1920 as the IRA, under the leadership of Michael Collins, mounted widespread attacks against the British administration.

In response to these attacks, the British government embarked on a policy of reinforcement, recruiting thousands of World War I veterans into the Royal Irish Constabulary, creating a force that came to be known infamously as the 'Black and Tans.' These auxiliary forces were notorious for their brutal tactics, including reprisals against civilians and the destruction of towns, which fueled greater animosity and resistance among the Irish populace.

Perhaps one of the most pivotal events of 1920 was 'Bloody Sunday,' on November 21. This day saw a coordinated IRA operation led by Collins, which targeted British intelligence officers in Dublin, resulting in the death of fourteen officers. In a violent reprisal on the same day, British forces killed fourteen civilians when they opened fire at a Gaelic football match at Croke Park. This day of bloodshed further escalated the conflict and provoked widespread international condemnation.

While violence escalated on the streets, significant developments were also occurring in the political sphere. The year 1920 saw the enactment of the Government of Ireland Act by the British parliament, aiming to establish Home Rule in Ireland by creating two separate parliaments, one for Northern Ireland and one for Southern Ireland. However, this Act was rejected by Irish nationalists who sought complete independence for the whole of Ireland.

In the midst of violence and political maneuvering, 1920 was also a year of local resistance and community organization. In an act of defiance against British rule, the Irish population elected Sinn Féin representatives, who established the underground Irish

Republic. Courts, local councils, and police were all organized under this extra-legal government, further solidifying the Irish commitment to independence.

Thus, 1920 stood as a defining year in the Irish War of Independence. A year that saw the courage of a nation seeking autonomy amid the specter of retaliation and amidst political complexity. It was a testament to Ireland's indomitable spirit, echoing the broader theme of 1920 - a year of global upheaval, resistance, and change.

CHAPTER 5: THE DAWN OF THE CHINESE CIVIL WAR - IDEOLOGIES AT ODDS

The year 1920 marked a period of dramatic sociopolitical changes globally, and nowhere was this more evident than in the heart of Asia. In China, a nascent struggle between conflicting ideologies was burgeoning, setting the stage for what would eventually become one of the longest and bloodiest conflicts of the 20th century - the Chinese Civil War.

The Chinese Civil War was primarily a conflict between the Nationalist Party, or Kuomintang (KMT), led by Sun Yat-sen and later Chiang Kai-shek, and the Communist Party of China (CPC), commanded by Chen Duxiu and Li Dazhao, with notable figures like Mao Zedong rising to prominence later. While the full-scale war did not erupt until 1927, the seeds of discord were undeniably sown in the 1920s.

By the start of 1920, the Qing Dynasty's fall in 1912 had led to a decade of upheaval, culminating in a highly fragmented state ruled by regional warlords. The year was marked by the absence of a strong central government and an increasing sense of national frustration at the inability to stave off foreign intervention and exploitation.

In this tumultuous environment, the two leading political factions, the KMT and CPC, emerged as potential national unifiers. Sun Yat-sen, who had been instrumental in overthrowing the Qing Dynasty, became the leader of the KMT, which was initially dedicated to implementing a democratic system in China based on the Three Principles of the People: nationalism, democracy, and social welfare.

Contrastingly, the CPC was formally founded in 1921 by Chen Duxiu and Li Dazhao, who had become increasingly influenced by Marxist-Leninist ideologies. Their aspiration was to construct a communist state modeled after the Soviet Union's governance, envisioning a society where class distinctions were abolished and wealth was distributed equitably.

However, the year 1920 was less about the direct conflict between these two political factions and more about their individual growth and attempts to gain support. The KMT sought to unify the country by consolidating the power of various warlords under their banner. Sun Yat-sen initiated the Northern Expedition in an attempt to unify the nation under the KMT's rule.

The CPC, on the other hand, began making inroads among the urban proletariat and intellectual classes in 1920. They disseminated Marxist-Leninist ideologies through publications and lectures, gaining traction among individuals dissatisfied with the existing power structure and foreign interference.

As a testament to the extraordinary complexity of this period, it's worth noting that these two ideological rivals initially formed a united front against the warlords in 1923 under the advisement of the Comintern - the international communist organization led by the Soviet Union. This somewhat uneasy alliance was reflective of the political maneuvering and pragmatic strategy that characterized this era.

In conclusion, 1920 was the dawn of a complex struggle in China, one that would erupt into a full-blown civil war only a few years later. It was a year of nascent ideological conflict, the growth of rival political factions, and the increasing awareness of the Chinese people that a struggle for the nation's very identity was on the horizon. The echoes of this struggle resonate through China's modern history, tracing its roots back to this pivotal year.

CHAPTER 6: WOMEN'S SUFFRAGE - THE RATIFICATION OF THE 19TH AMENDMENT

The year 1920 was a momentous one for women in the United States. The confirmation of the 19th Amendment on August 18, 1920, banned the states and the federal government from preventing citizens having the right to vote on the basis of sex, thus marking a significant milestone in the long battle for women's suffrage.

The Women's Suffrage Movement in the United States, which had been gradually gaining momentum since the mid-19th century, experienced its triumphant culmination in 1920. However, it's important to understand this achievement was not the result of a sudden wave of enlightenment in 1920 but rather the outcome of a protracted and often contentious struggle fought by determined suffragettes who refused to have their voices silenced.

At the dawn of the 1920s, women in several states had already secured the right to vote. However, the movement's ultimate aim was a constitutional amendment that would guarantee this right nationwide. After decades of lobbying, marching, and protesting, the suffragettes' efforts finally bore fruit when the 19th

Amendment, initially proposed in 1878, was passed by Congress on June 4, 1919. It then proceeded to the critical stage of state ratification.

Over a year-long period, one by one, the states began voting in favor of the Amendment. Tennessee became the pivotal 36th state to ratify the Amendment on August 18, 1920, providing the necessary three-fourths majority required for the Amendment's adoption. An infamous anecdote from this era involves Harry T. Burn, a young Tennessee legislator, who, influenced by a letter from his mother urging him to "be a good boy" and vote for the Amendment, switched his vote, thus ensuring its ratification.

The ratification of the 19th Amendment heralded a new era of political engagement for women. For the first time, millions of women across the United States had the opportunity to cast their votes in the Presidential election of November 1920, shifting the dynamics of American politics.

Yet, it's essential to acknowledge the 19th Amendment as a significant but incomplete victory. While it legally granted women the right to vote, in practice, many women, particularly women of color, faced numerous barriers to voting, including literacy tests, poll taxes, and outright intimidation. It would take several more decades of struggle, and further legislation, like the Voting Rights Act of 1965, to extend the franchise more equitably.

In sum, 1920 witnessed a crucial advancement in women's rights in the United States, driven by the unwavering dedication of the suffragettes who championed the cause. The ratification of the 19th Amendment did more than just grant women the right to vote—it symbolized the increasing political, social, and economic agency of women, paving the way for further gender equality advancements throughout the century. As we reflect on this momentous year, we must remember the profound transformation that the power of the ballot brought about, not just for women but for the fabric of American democracy.

CHAPTER 7: THE PROHIBITION ERA BEGINS - A MORAL CRUSADE IN AMERICA

As the year 1920 unfolded, a significant sociopolitical transformation occurred in America that would forever mark the decade - the onset of Prohibition. The ratification of the 18th Amendment into the U.S. Constitution in January 1920, along with the Volstead Act, marked the commencement of the Prohibition era, banning the manufacture, sale, and transportation of intoxicating liquors. This law was not merely an act of legislation but a powerful moral crusade that sought to reshape American society.

Prohibition was largely the result of a complex mix of societal factors, including a rise in religious conservatism and the efforts of groups like the Women's Christian Temperance Union (WCTU) and the Anti-Saloon League (ASL). These groups, backed by various Protestant denominations, saw alcohol as the root cause of many societal issues, including domestic violence and poverty, and campaigned fervently for its ban.

As a result, at the dawn of the 18th Amendment, legal taverns and saloons across America closed their doors, fostering the illusion of a new era of temperance and morality. However, the reality was markedly different. The law's enforcement proved to be a formidable task, given the widespread public opposition and the lack of a comprehensive federal apparatus to implement it. It became increasingly clear that while the law could ban the liquor trade, it could not eliminate the demand for alcohol.

This led to an unprecedented rise in illegal activities, as speakeasies replaced saloons, and organized crime syndicates, such as the infamous Chicago outfit led by Al Capone, exploited the opportunity for illicit trade in bootleg alcohol. Home-brewing and the use of industrial alcohols also became commonplace, leading to numerous public health issues. Additionally, government corruption, as law enforcement officers were often bribed to ignore illegal activities, further undermined the effectiveness of Prohibition.

The onset of Prohibition also had significant economic implications. The government lost vital tax revenue from the alcohol industry while simultaneously spending heavily on law enforcement. The legal alcohol industry, a significant employer, was devastated, leading to job losses and economic hardship for many.

Moreover, the enforcement of Prohibition accentuated social and cultural divisions. It became a point of contention between urban and rural, religious and secular, and immigrant and native-born Americans. Many recent immigrants, particularly those from wine-drinking countries like Italy and France, saw Prohibition as an affront to their cultural traditions.

Although Prohibition was implemented in 1920, its roots lay in the societal and political shifts of the late 19th and early 20th centuries, and its effects would reverberate throughout the 1920s and beyond. It was not merely a constitutional amendment but a societal experiment that reflected the complex interplay of morality, law, economics, and culture. Despite its noble intent, Prohibition ultimately illustrated the difficulties in legislating morality and the unanticipated consequences that often result from such attempts. As such, it remains an integral part of America's sociopolitical narrative in 1920, offering invaluable insights into the nation's cultural fabric during this period.

CHAPTER 8:
ECONOMIC UPHEAVAL
- THE DEPRESSIONS
AND RECOVERIES
POST-WAR

The aftermath of World War I ushered in an era of economic uncertainty, filled with cycles of depressions and recoveries, deeply affecting the global stage in 1920. The scale of the Great War had necessitated significant government borrowing, shifted industrial production, and dislocated international trade, all leading to the post-war economic tumult that is crucial to understanding the year 1920 and its place within the wider narrative of the 20th century.

In Europe, the end of the war brought about the deflation of the war economy. During the war years, the European powers had focused their economies on war production, which had supported employment and wages. However, the transition to peacetime in the late 1910s meant a sudden shift in demand away from military goods towards consumer products. This transition was anything but smooth, with the consequence that 1920 was a year marked by high unemployment rates and steeply falling prices, known as deflation, in many European countries.

Further complicating matters, Germany was saddled with hefty reparations outlined in the Treaty of Versailles, straining an already war-ravaged economy. The nation entered a period of hyperinflation, with the mark's value plummeting as the government printed money to meet its financial obligations. This instability would later provide fertile ground for radical political movements.

The United Kingdom, once the world's leading economic power, found itself laden with massive war debts, predominantly to the United States, which required significant budgetary changes and policy shifts to address. Coupled with the loss of manpower due to the war and a struggling colonial economy, the country experienced high unemployment rates and significant social unrest during this period.

In stark contrast, the United States emerged from the war relatively unscathed and in a robust economic position. The war years had seen a boom in American industry, transforming the country into the world's leading creditor nation. As Europe struggled, America experienced the beginning of an era known as the Roaring Twenties, marked by significant economic growth and rapid industrial development. However, even this growth was not without its issues. The year 1920 was marked by a brief but sharp recession, often referred to as the Depression of 1920-21, which saw a rapid rise in unemployment and a sharp contraction in output. Still, despite this downturn, the broader trajectory of the American economy was one of growth and expansion.

Asia, particularly Japan, also saw significant economic shifts in 1920. The Japanese economy, much like that of the United States, had greatly benefited from the war. Japan had stepped in to fill the manufacturing gap left by the warring European powers, leading to a rapid industrial expansion and an influx of wealth. However, the end of the war also meant an end to these favorable conditions, and Japan found itself facing an economic downturn in 1920, known as the Showa Financial Crisis.

Thus, the economic story of 1920 was one of upheaval and paradox, featuring both depressions and recoveries, where some countries ascended to new economic heights while others grappled with fiscal crises. These economic shifts significantly influenced the sociopolitical landscapes of these regions, contributing to the transformative changes that would define the rest of the decade and beyond. Understanding these financial ebbs and flows is crucial in comprehending the broader narrative of this pivotal year and the dramatic changes that lay ahead.

CHAPTER 9: THE BIRTH OF THE LEAGUE OF NATIONS - THE HOPE FOR COLLECTIVE SECURITY

As the world grappled with the social, political, and economic aftermath of the Great War, the dawn of 1920 marked a new chapter in the pursuit of global peace: the birth of the League of Nations. The League emerged as the centerpiece of U.S. President Woodrow Wilson's Fourteen Points, which laid the groundwork for peace negotiations and the Treaty of Versailles in 1919. On the date of January 10, 1920, the League of Nations officially came into existence, promising a new era of collective security and international cooperation.

The League was born from the ashes of World War I, its creation driven by the desire to prevent such catastrophic warfare from recurring. It was an ambitious experiment in global governance, representing the world's first intergovernmental organization of its scale, predating the United Nations by more than two decades. Its principal mission was to maintain international peace and resolve disputes among nations through diplomacy and negotiation rather than warfare.

This new international organization's covenant outlined the mechanisms through which the League would foster international cooperation and prevent conflicts. It included procedures for peaceful conflict resolution, disarmament, and sanctions against aggressive nations. The League also involved itself in a variety of social and economic issues, aiming to improve global health, labor conditions, refugee crises, and more. The League's broad mandate represented an ambitious vision for a new kind of global politics that prioritized peace and diplomacy over military force.

The membership of the League of Nations grew rapidly, beginning with the 42 founding members in 1920. By the mid-1920s, nearly 60 countries had joined the League, representing a broad swath of the world's nations. However, notably absent from the League's membership was the United States, despite President Wilson's instrumental role in its creation. The U.S. Congress rejected the Treaty of Versailles and, with it, the covenant of the League of Nations, a decision driven by concerns over national sovereignty and fears of being drawn into future European conflicts.

Despite this setback, the League started its work in earnest. Its first assembly was held in November 1920 in Geneva, Switzerland. The League tackled numerous international disputes in its early years and made strides in areas like global health and workers' rights. However, its inability to enforce its resolutions and the lack of participation from several major powers were deficiencies that would ultimately challenge its efficacy and longevity.

The birth of the League of Nations in 1920 represented an unprecedented step towards an organized international community, a step driven by the horrors of World War I and a widespread desire to ensure that such a catastrophe would never recur. The League embodied a vision for a world governed by diplomacy and cooperation rather than conflict and warfare. Although the League's life was fraught with challenges, and it ultimately could not prevent the onset of World War II, its creation signified a major milestone in the history of international relations, the echoes of which can still be seen in our global institutions today.

CHAPTER 10: THE EXPANSION OF RADIO - THE START OF A COMMUNICATION REVOLUTION

One cannot overlook the significance of 1920 in the history of mass communication. This was the year that marked the dawn of the radio era, a technological revolution that transformed global communication and information dissemination.

The roots of radio date back to the 19th century, with inventors such as Guglielmo Marconi and Nikola Tesla laying the groundwork for wireless communication. However, it was not until the second decade of the 20th century that radio technology would truly come into its own. Radio's great leap forward came in the United States, with Pittsburgh's KDKA being the first commercially licensed radio station. On November 2, 1920, KDKA made the first broadcast in history, covering the U.S. presidential election. The station relayed results live as they came in, a novelty that fascinated listeners and set a precedent for how breaking news could be reported.

The impact of this new medium was immediate and profound. For the first time, news could be disseminated quickly and broadly, reaching the public almost instantaneously. This immediacy brought about a profound shift in the public consciousness. With radio, people could learn about and connect with events happening far beyond their immediate geographical surroundings. They could be part of a shared national or even global experience, fostering a sense of unity and collective identity.

Beyond news, radio opened up vast new channels for entertainment. Dramas, comedies, and musical programs became staples of the airwaves, offering a communal experience that brought together families and communities. Notably, the popularity of jazz music discussed further in Chapter 12, was significantly boosted by radio broadcasts.

Despite the rapid adoption and popularity of radio, the technology was not without its challenges. In the early years, radio faced regulatory hurdles and technical limitations. The quality of the sound was often poor, and the broadcasting range was limited. However, these challenges did not curb the enthusiasm for the medium, and advancements over the subsequent decades would address many of these issues.

In terms of societal impact, radio played an integral role in the democratization of information. News and entertainment were no longer exclusive to the urban elite, and literacy was not a prerequisite for access to information. The egalitarian potential of radio cannot be overstated, as it made information accessible to the masses, irrespective of social status or geographic location.

The expansion of radio in 1920 initiated a seismic shift

in the landscape of mass communication. This technology, which allowed for instantaneous dissemination of news and entertainment, revolutionized how society consumed information and fostered a sense of shared experience among listeners. Radio not only reshaped the media landscape but also had significant societal and cultural implications, shaping the roaring twenties and the decades that followed. This chapter of 1920 represents the birth of a new era in mass communication, setting the stage for the dynamic, interconnected world we inhabit today.

CHAPTER 11: SILENT FILMS - THE GOLDEN AGE OF HOLLYWOOD

In the annals of cinematic history, 1920 holds a unique and pivotal position. This year heralded the onset of the golden age of Hollywood, with the silent film era reaching its zenith. A potent blend of artistic innovation, star power, and emerging industry trends, these early silent films laid the groundwork for the dominant cultural medium of the 20th century and beyond.

From the start, silent films were a multinational affair. Europe, especially France, Germany, and Italy, had initially dominated the global film industry. But the devastation of World War I disrupted the European film industry, providing an opportunity for the American film industry to gain ascendency. The epicenter of this boom was Hollywood, California. By 1920, Hollywood was producing the majority of films in the world, a trend that would continue for decades.

While the language of silent film was universal, the stories they told were undeniably influenced by the era's sociopolitical landscape. The upheaval and disillusionment of the post-war years were evident in the screenplays of the time. It was a period of transition and transformation, and the silent films of 1920 mirrored this turbulence while also providing an escape from it.

One of the most remarkable aspects of the silent film era was the birth of the Hollywood star system. 1920 was a defining year for the careers of numerous screen icons. Silent film luminaries such as Charlie Chaplin, Buster Keaton, and Mary Pickford had already established themselves in the industry, but 1920 saw their popularity skyrocket. Their talent and charisma combined with clever marketing tactics to create a star-driven culture that remains a Hollywood staple.

This year also marked the premiere of Robert J. Flaherty's "Nanook of the North," often considered the first feature-length documentary. The film, chronicling the life of an Inuit man in the Canadian Arctic, highlighted the capacity of film to inform and educate, establishing a genre that would come to hold significant sway in the world of cinema.

Alongside the rise of stars and genres, 1920 saw the development of the studio system, with production companies like Paramount, Warner Bros., and Universal Pictures gaining dominance. These studios wielded immense power, controlling every aspect of film production, distribution, and exhibition, setting the stage for the "Golden Age of Hollywood."

Notably, this was also a time of technological innovation. Although films were silent, this did not equate to a lack of sophistication. Cinematographers experimented with lighting and camera angles, and film directors explored the potential of visual storytelling, creating rich narratives that didn't need words for their expression.

The silent film era of 1920, the dawn of Hollywood's golden age, was more than an entertainment revolution. It was a phenomenon that mirrored and influenced societal changes in a world emerging from war. These silent narratives, acting as visual chronicles, projected human experiences, hopes, and fears onto the silver screen, reaching millions across the globe. As we reflect on the cultural history of the 20th century, the silent films of 1920 offer a unique lens, capturing the zeitgeist of a world in transition.

CHAPTER 12: JAZZ AGE - THE MUSIC OF THE ROARING TWENTIES

As the 1920s roared into life, so did its soundtrack. This period, famously dubbed the Jazz Age, was one in which music, particularly jazz, wove a powerful spell over society. Jazz music, a melodic cocktail of African rhythms, blues tonality, and European harmonic structure, had emerged from the melting pot of New Orleans in the late 19th and early 20th century. By 1920, it had begun its symphonic conquest of the United States and, soon after, the world.

The year 1920 was a pivot point for jazz, witnessing significant evolutions in both the musical form itself and its societal impact. The jazz of this time was a reflection of the era: dynamic, daring, and rife with innovations. A key shift was the transition from collective improvisation, where all musicians played simultaneously, to a style that featured soloists more prominently. This evolution allowed for virtuosic performers to emerge, bringing with them a new era of instrumental prowess and personal expression.

These artistic developments were mirrored by and interconnected with broader societal changes. The widespread migration of African Americans from the rural South to the urban North during the Great Migration brought jazz to new audiences. Chicago and New York became significant hubs, fostering their own distinctive jazz scenes. The music found fertile ground in these cosmopolitan centers, intertwining with the social and cultural fabric of urban life. Jazz became a symbol of the new modernity, expressing the energy, complexity, and dynamism of the Roaring Twenties.

1920 was a landmark year for the jazz recording industry. The first jazz recordings had appeared just a few years prior, but the technology was still in its infancy, and the quality of these early records was often poor. But technical advancements in recording during this time improved sound quality and fidelity, helping to boost the popularity of recorded jazz music. The release of Mamie Smith's "Crazy Blues" in 1920, often hailed as the first blues recording, sold a staggering one million copies in its first six months, signaling a new commercial viability for African American music.

The proliferation of the radio, discussed in Chapter 10, also played a crucial role in jazz's 1920 explosion. Radio stations began to broadcast jazz performances live, enabling the music to reach a far wider audience than ever before. Jazz became a national phenomenon, consumed by a diverse cross-section of American society.

Despite its burgeoning popularity, jazz was not without controversy. Its association with the nightlife, speakeasies, and the perceived loosening of moral standards led to disapproval from more conservative corners of society. The music became a focal point for debates about race, class, and the very nature of American identity. Yet, these debates only fueled its fame and influence further.

In its embrace of improvisation and individual expression, jazz embodied the spirit of the age: the thirst for innovation, the break with tradition, and the restless energy of a society in transition. Through its seductive rhythms and harmonic complexities, it articulated the joy, pain, and contradictions of life in this tumultuous period. The Jazz Age was more than just a musical epoch; it was a social and cultural revolution that had its roots firmly planted in the year 1920. And as the world danced to this new rhythm, the face of music and modern culture was irrevocably changed.

CHAPTER 13: THE FLAPPER MOVEMENT - WOMEN'S FASHION AND FREEDOM

In the annals of fashion history, few figures are as iconic as the Flapper. Synonymous with the Roaring Twenties, the Flapper embodied a new breed of women who were challenging traditional notions of femininity, societal roles, and freedom. The year 1920 marked a significant milestone in the genesis of this cultural movement, playing host to the conditions that allowed flapper culture to flourish.

The flapper style was defined by a distinctive aesthetic. Women adorned themselves in knee-length skirts with a shift-style silhouette, a stark contrast to the restrictive corsets and long, full-bodied dresses of the Victorian era. Their hair was typically cut short in a bob style, again defying the conventional norms that equated long hair with feminine beauty. The use of makeup became more widespread, along with accessories such as long pearl necklaces, cloche hats, and ornate headbands. This new style was not merely about fashion but a bold statement of autonomy and modernity.

The roots of the flapper movement can be traced back to the

societal upheavals during and after World War I. The war had fundamentally altered the role of women in society, as they had taken up positions in the workforce while men were at the front lines. By 1920, these experiences had begun to reshape societal expectations and attitudes about women's roles. The ratification of the 19th Amendment in the United States, granting women the right to vote, was a monumental victory that boosted the burgeoning movement.

The flapper ethos wasn't just about fashion; it was about behavior and attitudes as well. Flappers were seen as young, single women who relished their independence and indulged in activities that were once considered solely the domain of men. They smoked, drank, drove cars, and openly participated in the vibrant nightlife. They engaged in casual dating and expressed a candid attitude towards sexuality, challenging the restrictive morals of the time.

Jazz music, as discussed in the previous chapter, was the rhythm to which the Flapper danced. The vibrant and dynamic music became the soundtrack of their rebellion, an emblem of the modern culture they were helping to shape. The Jazz Age and the flapper movement were symbiotic cultural phenomena, each fueling the energy and spirit of the other.

Yet, flapper culture was met with mixed reactions. Traditionalists saw them as a threat to the moral order, with their flamboyant behavior and disregard for established norms. Their critics accused them of being superficial and morally loose. However, flappers saw themselves differently. They represented a new woman, unbound and unencumbered, living their lives on their own terms.

The flapper movement was not just an American phenomenon. The liberated image of the Flapper resonated with women across the Atlantic in Europe as well, adding to the cultural dialogue that was sweeping across nations. The movement played a vital role in changing societal norms, contributing to the evolution of women's rights, and forever transforming fashion and popular culture.

1920 was the year when the seeds of this transformative movement truly began to germinate. The Flapper, with her bobbed hair and shorter skirts, her love for jazz and the nightlife, became a symbol of the era. More than a mere fashion trend, the Flapper embodied the spirit of the Roaring Twenties, symbolizing a generation's aspiration for freedom, fun, and a break from the past.

CHAPTER 14: TECHNOLOGICAL INNOVATIONS - GROWTH OF AVIATION AND AUTOMOTIVE INDUSTRIES

The year 1920 was not just significant for its sociopolitical changes and cultural shifts; it also marked a notable acceleration in technological innovations, particularly within the aviation and automotive industries. The rapid advancements in these fields changed the ways in which people and goods moved across the globe, setting the stage for the modern world as we know it.

The decade following the end of World War I saw an unprecedented boom in aviation. The war had propelled significant advancements in aircraft design and production, and these military technologies were quickly repurposed for commercial and civilian use after the conflict ended. By 1920, the potential of aviation as a means of transportation was beginning to be recognized.

In the United States, the first regular airmail service had begun as early as 1918, and by 1920, it was steadily expanding. The passage of the Kelly Act in 1925 would later fully privatize this service, paving the way for today's commercial airlines. Across the Atlantic, similar developments were occurring. In 1920, KLM, the world's oldest airline still operating under its original name, was founded in the Netherlands.

While these were significant developments, it's important to note that aviation in 1920 was still in its infancy. Commercial passenger flights were rare, and aviation was viewed by many as a risky endeavor. However, the advancements of this period laid the groundwork for the growth of commercial aviation over the subsequent decades.

Parallel to these advancements in aviation, the automotive industry was also undergoing a major transformation in 1920. The Model T, introduced by Henry Ford in 1908, had revolutionized the automobile industry by providing a relatively affordable motor vehicle for the middle class. By 1920, the effects of this revolution were visible across the United States and Western Europe.

Cars were no longer the exclusive domain of the wealthy elite; they had become attainable for a broader segment of the population. This was largely due to the efficiencies created by the assembly line production method, another innovation popularized by Henry Ford. This method reduced costs and allowed for mass production, making the car a common feature in many households.

Furthermore, the impact of the automotive industry extended beyond the car itself. It stimulated growth in other sectors, such as steel, rubber, and glass, which were all necessary for car production. It also led to the development of a nationwide infrastructure of roads, bridges, and highways, which reshaped the physical landscape of many countries.

Moreover, the growth of the automotive industry revolutionized societal norms. It enabled greater mobility, leading to the growth of suburban areas as people could commute longer distances to work. This increased mobility also allowed for greater leisure opportunities, fundamentally transforming the ways in which people lived and worked.

1920 was a year of transformation and change on many fronts, and the growth of the aviation and automotive industries were key facets of this. These technological advancements set in motion trends that would profoundly shape the course of the 20th century, affecting not only the economy but also the societal, cultural, and geographical makeup of nations around the world.

CHAPTER 15: THE WALL STREET BOMBING - THE RISE OF DOMESTIC TERRORISM

The rise of the 1920s was not without its violent disruptions, casting a dark shadow over the promise of the Roaring Twenties. On September 16, 1920, an act of terrorism rocked the financial heart of the United States – the Wall Street district in New York City. The bombing of Wall Street was one of the earliest acts of large-scale domestic terrorism on American soil and a grim testament to the sociopolitical turbulence of the era.

Just after noon on that fateful day, a horse-drawn cart packed with explosives and iron slugs detonated outside the J.P. Morgan Bank on Wall Street. The blast instantly claimed dozens of lives, and the death toll eventually rose to 38. Hundreds more were injured, and nearby buildings were severely damaged, including the U.S. Treasury's Assay Office and the J.P. Morgan building itself.

The Wall Street bombing was a stark manifestation of the political tensions that had been simmering beneath the surface of American society. These tensions were fueled by a variety of factors, including economic instability, labor unrest, and the ideological clashes of the post-World War I era. Some historians and contemporaries suspected anarchists or radical socialists who were active during this time and who had previously used bombings as a method of protest.

Despite a three-year investigation by the Bureau of Investigation (BOI), the precursor to the FBI, the perpetrators were never identified, and the case officially remains unsolved. Theories abound regarding who was responsible for the bombing, with some pointing fingers at Italian anarchists, in particular, a group led by Luigi Galleani.

The Wall Street bombing represented an abrupt interruption to the narrative of prosperity and progress that characterized the early 1920s. It served as a stark reminder of the unresolved social and political tensions in the United States and signaled the emergence of a new form of political expression: domestic terrorism. This horrifying event put the nation on notice that despite the optimism and exuberance of the era, the Roaring Twenties also had a darker, more volatile side.

The bombing marked a turning point in the nation's approach to political violence and security. The government's response was marked by an increase in surveillance of suspected radicals and a greater focus on domestic security. The Wall Street bombing played a pivotal role in the early development of the FBI, shaping its emerging focus on political violence and domestic terrorism. In effect, the bombing served as a grim harbinger of the challenges that lay ahead for law enforcement and national security agencies in the 20th century and beyond.

Indeed, the bombing was indicative of the broader societal

tension of the era, a reflection of the growing pains that came with the transition into a modern, urbanized society. As the United States grappled with these internal struggles, this domestic terrorism event became a part of the complex tapestry of 1920, furthering the narrative of the tumultuous aftermath of the Great War and the sociopolitical changes in the post-war world.

CHAPTER 16:
THE MEXICAN
REVOLUTION - THE
END OF A CIVIL WAR

The Mexican Revolution, a conflict that began in 1910, had finally come to a significant turning point by the dawn of 1920. In this chapter, we delve into this tumultuous era of Mexican history, marked by political strife, economic challenges, and societal upheaval. A narrative dominated by key figures and turning events, this was a pivotal period that reshaped the destiny of Mexico, promising reform and social justice.

The year 1920 witnessed the end of a decade-long struggle, the Mexican Revolution - one of the most critical periods in Mexico's history. It saw the dramatic fall of President Venustiano Carranza, which effectively put an end to the fighting and marked a new beginning in Mexican political life.

Carranza had managed to maintain a firm grip on power since 1917 by controlling the constitutionalist faction of the revolution. However, his presidency was plagued with controversies and conflicts. One significant contentious point was his policy towards labor, especially his reluctance to implement agrarian reforms promised in the Constitution of 1917, sparking discontent among the peasantry and working classes.

Carranza's decision to impose his chosen successor, Ignacio Bonillas, in the 1920 elections was the last straw that triggered the Plan of Agua Prieta, a political manifesto and military plan adopted by the Sonoran revolutionary leaders, including Alvaro Obregon, Plutarco Elías Calles, and Adolfo de la Huerta. This plan denounced Carranza's government and called for an armed revolt, a call which quickly garnered widespread support.

In May 1920, Carranza was ousted from the presidency, leading to his eventual death. Adolfo de la Huerta became interim president and oversaw the election of Álvaro Obregón later in the year. Obregón's presidency marked the beginning of a period of relative stability and the implementation of much-needed reforms, many of which had been promised in the 1917 constitution but had yet to be enacted.

Obregon's presidency brought a significant shift in government policy. He was instrumental in implementing agrarian reforms, providing land rights to the peasants, and pushing for labor laws that improved working conditions. These measures helped to soothe the social tensions that had fueled the revolution and set Mexico on a new path of development and modernization.

Yet, despite these advancements, the end of the Mexican Revolution in 1920 did not immediately solve all of the country's problems. The new government faced a daunting task: to reconstruct a country devastated by ten years of civil war, to unite various factions under a single national government, and to fulfill the social and economic promises of the revolution.

1920 was a pivotal year for Mexico, marking the end of

a destructive civil war and the beginning of a challenging process of national reconstruction and transformation. It was a turning point that shaped Mexico's political, social, and economic structures, making the year an integral part of the broader narrative of the post-war world's sociopolitical changes. It reaffirmed the principle that the aftermath of conflict can be a catalyst for change, leading to reform and the rebuilding of a more equitable society.

CHAPTER 17: ART AND LITERATURE - THE LOST GENERATION AND THE DADA MOVEMENT

The year 1920, a watershed moment for the world, was no less significant in the realm of art and literature. The post-war period, a tumultuous maelstrom of change, bore witness to the genesis of new artistic expressions and literary movements that challenged the traditional norms and dared to question the established order. This chapter turns the spotlight on two influential movements that emerged from the ashes of World War I: the Lost Generation of Writers and the Dada art movement.

The term' Lost Generation,' coined by Gertrude Stein and popularized by Ernest Hemingway, refers to the disillusioned youth who survived the Great War. These individuals, the young men and women of the 1920s, were characterized by their disillusionment with societal norms, their loss of faith in the American Dream, and their struggle to find meaning in a world scarred by war.

Members of the Lost Generation, including notable writers such as Hemingway, F. Scott Fitzgerald, and T.S. Eliot, questioned the values of their society in their works, presenting a stark contrast to the pre-war idealistic literature. Their narratives often depicted individuals alienated from society, grappling with moral and psychological issues, and searching for meaning in a seemingly absurd world. They shed light on the angst and disillusionment of a generation caught between the shadow of a horrific past and an uncertain future.

Parallel to the emergence of the Lost Generation in literature, the world of art saw the birth of the Dada movement. Originating in Zurich, Switzerland, during the height of World War I, Dada was a form of artistic anarchy born out of the revulsion for the senseless violence of war. By 1920, it had spread to cities such as Berlin, Cologne, New York, and Paris, each with its own unique take on the movement.

Dada art was a radical departure from conventional aesthetics. It defied reason, logic, and standard artistic methods. The artists used various media, including collage, sound, and abstract forms, to communicate their disdain for the perceived rationality that had led to the war. Notable figures in the Dada movement included Marcel Duchamp, Tristan Tzara, and Max Ernst. Their art was a rebellious response to the horrors of war, echoing the larger societal shift towards questioning and challenging established norms.

The Lost Generation and the Dada movement, born of the same disillusionment and dissatisfaction, were artistic responses to the turmoil and trauma of World War I. They were symbols of resistance, manifestations of a generation's attempt to reconcile with a world that had lost its sense of certainty and order. These movements held a mirror to the stark realities of the post-war world, capturing the zeitgeist of a transformative era.

In retrospect, the Lost Generation and the Dada movement marked a pivotal point in the evolution of 20th-century art and literature. Their profound influence is still felt today, a testament to the enduring power of art and literature to reflect, respond to, and shape the course of human history. The year 1920 was a critical juncture in this creative journey, a time when the rubble of a war-torn world gave birth to new narratives and avant-garde expressions, challenging and reshaping our understanding of art, literature, and society.

CHAPTER 18: SCIENCE AND MEDICINE - ADVANCES IN THE WAKE OF THE SPANISH FLU

The year 1920 marked the twilight of the Spanish flu pandemic, a catastrophic health crisis that decimated populations worldwide between 1918 and 1920. With an estimated 50 million deaths, the pandemic served as a sobering reminder of the vulnerabilities of human society in the face of biological threats. However, it also catalyzed significant advancements in the fields of science and medicine. This chapter will delve into these consequential developments and their enduring impact.

The Spanish flu spurred governments and medical institutions to prioritize public health infrastructure. The pressing need for coordinated responses to health crises led to the creation of the League of Nations Health Organisation in 1920. As the precursor to today's World Health Organisation, it represented the recognition that global health challenges required international cooperation and standardized health policies.

Meanwhile, the pandemic underscored the critical need for scientific research into infectious diseases. In this respect, the influenza virus itself posed a significant challenge. Despite the severity of the Spanish flu, the exact nature of the pathogen responsible remained unknown in 1920. The virus wouldn't be identified until 1933, a delay indicative of the relatively nascent state of virology at the time.

The urgency created by the pandemic fueled advancements in the field. Scientists made strides in understanding the nature of viruses and how they differ from bacteria, critical knowledge for developing treatments. In 1920, the concept of a viral infection was still being refined, and this decade marked an inflection point in the field of virology, paving the way for later breakthroughs.

The pandemic also highlighted the necessity for vaccine research. Despite vaccines' existence for diseases like smallpox, the science was still in its early stages. The Spanish flu ignited a concerted effort to develop a vaccine for influenza, a challenging endeavor due to the virus's ability to mutate. This drive for a flu vaccine marked the start of a century-long quest that would yield sporadic success and recurring setbacks but would ultimately provide essential knowledge for combating influenza and other viral diseases.

In parallel, the period following the Spanish flu saw significant progress in other scientific disciplines. Physics was being revolutionized by Albert Einstein's theory of relativity and quantum mechanics. These breakthroughs challenged and redefined perceptions of the natural world, shaping the course of scientific inquiry throughout the 20th century and beyond.

In retrospect, the year 1920, while signifying the end of a

devastating pandemic, also marked a new dawn in science and medicine. The Spanish flu, for all its destruction, ignited an era of unprecedented scientific progress and underscored the intrinsic connection between global health and international cooperation. The innovations and advancements born from this challenging period are a testament to humanity's resilience and relentless pursuit of knowledge, echoing the broader themes of transition, evolution, and innovation that characterize the year 1920 in the annals of history.

CHAPTER 19: IMMIGRATION ACT OF 1920 - A SHIFT IN AMERICA'S DEMOGRAPHICS

1920 was a year marked by global transition and internal flux. In the United States, the sociopolitical landscape was evolving, reflecting not only the country's emergence as a global power but also the shifting demographic makeup of its population. One pivotal development in this narrative was the passage of the Immigration Act of 1920, also known as the Dillingham-Burnett Act, named after its principal architects, Vermont Senator William P. Dillingham and South Carolina Senator Nathan E. Burnett.

The Act represented a significant shift in America's approach to immigration. Its passage was the culmination of decades of nativist sentiment precipitated by changing patterns of immigration. Prior to the 1880s, the majority of immigrants to America were from Northern and Western Europe. However, from the 1890s onwards, a new wave of immigrants began arriving from Southern and Eastern Europe, who were often viewed with suspicion and prejudice due to their linguistic, religious, and cultural differences.

Under the Act, a literacy test was imposed on all immigrants over sixteen years of age. They had to demonstrate basic reading comprehension in their native language. Although it may seem benign, the literacy test was primarily designed to restrict the influx of new immigrants originating from Southern and Eastern Europe, most of whom had little formal education.

The Act also implemented a "quota system," which capped the number of immigrants from each country based on the nationality of the U.S. population according to the 1910 census. This system was explicitly designed to favor immigrants from Northern and Western Europe and limit those from Southern and Eastern Europe.

The passage of the Act was met with intense debate. Supporters argued that it was necessary to protect American jobs and maintain the nation's cultural identity. Detractors, on the other hand, criticized it as discriminatory and xenophobic, arguing that it was contrary to the nation's founding ideals as a beacon of opportunity and refuge.

The repercussions of the Immigration Act of 1920 were substantial. It effectively slowed the flow of immigration from certain regions, leading to a marked shift in the ethnic composition of immigrants to the United States. It also reinforced nativist sentiment and set a precedent for restrictive immigration policies, including the more draconian Immigration Act of 1924, which further limited immigration from Eastern and Southern Europe.

Despite the controversy surrounding its passage and legacy,

the Immigration Act of 1920 undeniably had a significant impact on the demographic and cultural makeup of the United States. It reflects the ongoing struggle to balance the nation's identity as a land of immigrants and the challenges posed by integration and multiculturalism. As we delve into the nuances of this transformative year, the Act serves as a critical lens through which we can understand the broader sociopolitical undercurrents that shaped America and the world during this period of transition.

CHAPTER 20: THE BIRTH OF MODERN SPORTS - BOXING, BASEBALL, AND THE OLYMPICS

In the tumultuous year of 1920, the world was not just shifting politically and socially but also culturally. One such facet was the evolution of modern sports. The aftermath of the Great War had left societies fractured, and sports provided an avenue for collective healing and unity. Three sporting phenomena of 1920, in particular, stand out for their influence and lasting impact: the rise of professional boxing and baseball in America and the seventh iteration of the modern Olympic Games.

Boxing in 1920 entered a golden era. In the post-war period, public interest in boxing swelled, and the sport was further legitimized by a well-regulated professional structure. A significant highlight was the heavyweight championship fight between Jack Dempsey and Bill Brennan. Dempsey, known as the "Manassa Mauler," was an explosive fighter whose raw power and ruthless aggression drew spectators. His successful defense of his title in December 1920 against Brennan in Madison Square Garden further solidified his status as a sporting icon.

Parallel to the boxing craze, baseball was captivating the American public. The year 1920 was pivotal due to the emergence of one George Herman "Babe" Ruth. Ruth, a former Boston Red Sox pitcher turned New York Yankees slugger, revolutionized the sport with his powerful and frequent home runs, an approach previously uncommon in baseball. Ruth's larger-than-life personality and extraordinary talent captured the nation's imagination, and his 54 home runs in the 1920 season broke records and ushered in what came to be known as baseball's "live-ball" era.

On the global stage, the 1920 Summer Olympics, held in Antwerp, Belgium, played a significant role in heralding the return of international camaraderie and competition in the aftermath of the war. The Games were noteworthy for their instances of triumph in the face of adversity, including the remarkable story of the American swimmer Ethelda Bleibtrey, who won three gold medals in spite of initially learning to swim while rehabilitating a broken leg.

Moreover, these Olympics marked the first appearance of the Olympic flag with the five interlocked rings, a symbol of global unity, representing the five inhabited continents of the world. It was also at these Games that the tradition of releasing doves as a symbol of peace began.

However, it's important to note that the spirit of unity was not absolute, as Germany, Austria, Hungary, Bulgaria, and the Ottoman Empire (collectively known as the Central Powers) were not invited due to their roles in World War I, reflecting the lingering political tensions of the era.

The influence of these sporting events extended far beyond

1920. The popularity of boxing and baseball skyrocketed, making sports a significant part of American cultural life. The Olympics, too, continued to grow as an international symbol of peaceful competition and unity among nations, despite underlying geopolitical strife. In a period of profound change and uncertainty, sports offered both a distraction from and a mirror to the world's broader sociopolitical landscape, weaving itself intricately into the cultural fabric of the Roaring Twenties.

CHAPTER 21: THE END OF THE YEAR - REFLECTIONS ON 1920

The year 1920 drew to a close as an epochal chapter in the unfolding narrative of the 20th century. It had been a year of dizzying change and stark contrasts, a year that combined groundbreaking advancements with destructive upheavals. The end of the year provided an opportunity for societies worldwide to pause and take stock of the transformation they had undergone.

In the political sphere, the echoes of the Great War continued to reverberate. The Treaty of Versailles and the League of Nations were the first steps toward a new international order, yet they also sowed the seeds for future conflict. The newly formed Soviet Union embarked on an ideological journey that promised to reshape world politics, while in the West, the ratification of the 19th Amendment in the United States marked a leap forward for women's rights.

Nations fought for their independence, as seen in Ireland and Mexico, while internal strife escalated into a civil war in China. In America, the Immigration Act sought to control the demographic shifts ignited by the post-war flux of immigrants. Economies around the world wrestled with depression and recovery, highlighting the interconnectedness and vulnerability of the global financial system.

Yet 1920 was not merely a year of political and economic upheaval. It was a year that marked significant shifts in culture and society. The Prohibition era began in America, altering social dynamics and spawning a wave of illicit activities. Advances in technology laid the foundation for modern communication, notably through the expansion of radio. Meanwhile, the silent films of Hollywood's Golden Age and the music of the Jazz Age offered new forms of entertainment and self-expression.

The style of the 'Flapper' embodied the changing role of women in society, while the world of sports echoed society's competitive spirit and need for communal engagement. Technological progress also saw leaps in the aviation and automotive industries, and despite the harsh lessons of the Spanish Flu, significant strides were made in science and medicine.

The world of art and literature reacted to the tumultuous times, giving birth to the Lost Generation and the Dada movement, capturing the zeitgeist of disillusionment and rejection of traditional norms. The Wall Street bombing was a grim reminder of the growth of domestic terrorism, another dark side to the rapid changes sweeping society.

As the year ended, the world had undeniably changed. Societies had been challenged, norms had been shattered, and the stage was set for the Roaring Twenties. There was a sense of anticipation mingled with anxiety. The world was evolving, and the events of 1920 had etched deep marks on the canvas of history. The implications of these changes would continue to unfold in the years that followed as the world propelled itself into a future filled with promise and uncertainty.

As we reflect on 1920, we can see it as a microcosm of the broader 20th century - an era of unprecedented change, marked by conflict and innovation, despair and hope, loss and discovery. The story of this year offers vital insights into the human capacity for resilience and adaptability in the face of relentless change. And in the tapestry of history, 1920 stands out as a vibrant and complex thread, a year that encapsulated the turmoil and triumph of the human spirit in a rapidly changing world.

CHAPTER 22: THE LASTING IMPACT OF 1920 - THE SEEDS OF OUR MODERN WORLD

The year 1920 holds a critical position in the annals of history, standing at the precipice of modernity while carrying the burdens of its recent past. It served as a prologue to the defining narratives of the 20th century, leaving enduring impressions on the world. This chapter examines the lasting impact of 1920, as the year's seismic shifts and significant developments still ripple through our contemporary existence.

The political terrain of 1920, marked by the birth of the Soviet Union, the conclusion of the Mexican Revolution, the Irish struggle for autonomy, and the dawn of the Chinese Civil War, significantly altered the global balance of power. These transitions, born from ideological conflict and the desire for national self-determination, reshaped international relations and laid the groundwork for geopolitical developments that would shape the rest of the century.

The ratification of the 19th Amendment in the United States reflected a broader global trend toward women's suffrage, paving the way for gender equality. This pivotal moment signaled the start of widespread societal recognition of women's rights, which continues to evolve and impact the world today.

Meanwhile, the U.S. Immigration Act of 1920, aimed at regulating the influx of immigrants, shaped the demographic destiny of the nation. It set a precedent for immigration policies that would define the cultural mosaic of America and, arguably, numerous other nations grappling with similar challenges.

Economic instability, characterized by the post-war depressions and recoveries, influenced financial systems worldwide. These upheavals precipitated a greater understanding of economic interdependencies, ultimately leading to the establishment of institutions designed to mitigate such instabilities.

In the realm of technology, the rapid expansion of radio and the growth of aviation and automotive industries signified the advent of the Communication Age and fast-paced transportation. These innovations revolutionized the way the world connected and moved, paving the way for the globally interconnected society we inhabit today.

Cultural shifts in 1920 also left a lasting legacy. The Prohibition era altered social norms and catalyzed significant changes in law enforcement and criminal activity, lessons of which inform current drug policy debates. Meanwhile, the emergence of the Jazz Age, silent films, the Flapper movement, and the Dada movement signified a cultural renaissance that transformed entertainment, fashion, and art - providing a basis for the diverse artistic and cultural expressions of the modern world.

In science and medicine, the aftermath of the Spanish Flu catalyzed significant advancements. The pandemic impressed upon the world the necessity for robust public health systems and disease surveillance protocols, cornerstones of modern medical practice.

Finally, the societal response to the Wall Street bombing of 1920, one of the first instances of large-scale domestic terrorism, led to enhanced security measures and investigation techniques. These developments, in a chilling echo, foreshadowed the ongoing struggle against domestic and international terrorism in the present century.

The year 1920 was a complex mosaic of events, movements, and developments that indelibly influenced the course of the 20th century and beyond. The era's tumultuous sociopolitical transitions, cultural shifts, technological advancements, and economic transformations continue to reverberate in our modern world. By studying this pivotal year, we gain critical insights into our contemporary challenges, reminding us of the intricate web of history that continually shapes our present and future.

THE END

Made in United States
Troutdale, OR
02/05/2025

28695463R00042